Excellence in English

Year 1

Preparation for Basic Skills Tests

Peter Howard

Peter Howard is an Australian ex-primary school principal and author of many text books and teaching aids. A number of his works are published in the UK, USA, Canada and Asian countries.

Excellence in English Year 1
© Peter Howard 2011
Published by Coroneos Publications 2011
First published 2011
ISBN 978-1-86294-235-6

This book is available from recognised booksellers or contact:

Coroneos Publications

Telephone: (02) 9838 9265   Facsimile: (02) 9838 8982
Business Address: 2/195 Prospect Highway Seven Hills 2147
Website: www.coroneos.com.au
E-mail: info@fivesenseseducation.com.au

Foreword

This workbook is the first of a six-book series. It is designed to give children a thorough grounding in the phonic approach to reading. This will enable them to move confidently to Level 2.

It is essential that a pupil works through the book progressively from the beginning to the end.

Answers are provided in a centre section, and may be easily removed. When using this book at home or school, it may be a temptation for a child to look at answers if they remain in the book.

Peter Howard

Contents

Beginning Sounds 1	6
Beginning Sounds 2	7
Beginning Sounds 3	8
Short Vowel Sound 'a'	9
Short Vowel Sound 'e'	10
Short Vowel Sound 'i'	11
Short Vowel Sound 'o'	12
Short Vowel Sound 'u'	13
Blending with 'a'	14
Blending with 'e'	15
Blending with 'i'	16
Blending with 'o'	17
Blending with 'u'	18
Ending with 'ck'	19
'ch' 'sh' 'th' and 'wh' Sounds	20
Long Vowel 'a'	21
Long Vowel 'i'	22
Long Vowel 'o'	23
Long Vowel 'u'	24
Double Sound 'ee'	25
Revision 'ee' Sound	26
Double Sound 'ea'	27
Revision 'ea' Sound	28
Short Double Sound 'oo'	29
Revision Short 'oo'	30
Long Double Sound 'oo'	31
Revision Long 'oo' Sound	32
Double Sound 'oa'	33

© **Peter Howard 2011   Published by Coroneos Publications**

Contents

Revision 'oa' Sound	34
Double Sound 'ow'	35
Revision 'ow' Sound	36
Double Sound 'or'	37
Revision 'or' Sound	38
Double Sound 'aw'	39
Revision 'aw' Sound	40
Double Sound 'ou'	41
Revision 'ou' Sound	42
Double Sound 'ow'	43
Revision 'ow' Sound	44
Double Sound 'ar'	45
Revision 'ar' Sound	46
Double Sound 'ai'	47
Revision 'ai' Sound	48
Double Sound 'ay'	49
Revision 'ay' Sound	50
Double Sound 'ir'	51
Revision 'ir' Sound	52
Double Sound 'ur'	53
Revision 'ur' Sound	54
Double Sound 'er'	55
Revision 'er' Sound	56
Harder Words 1	57
Harder Words 2	58
Harder Words 3	59
Harder Words 4	60

Beginning Sounds 1

Write the missing letter and the whole word again twice.

a for ant ......nt ....

b for bus ......us ....

c for cat ......at ....

d for dog ......og ....

e for egg ......gg ....

f for fan ......n ....

g for gun ......un ....

h for hat ......at ....

i for ink ......nk ....

Write the correct word next to each picture.

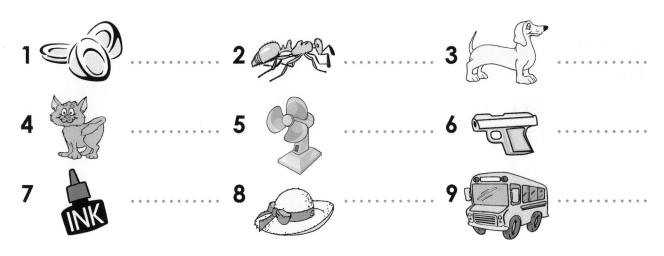

1 .... 2 .... 3 ....

4 .... 5 .... 6 ....

7 .... 8 .... 9 ....

    © Peter Howard 2011   Published by Coroneos Publications

Write the missing letter and the whole word again twice.

j for jet ......et ....

k for king ......ing ....

l for log ......og ....

m for man ......an ....

n for nut ......ut ....

o for ox ......x ....

p for pig ......ig ....

q for queen ......ueen ....

r for rat ......at ....

Write the correct word next to each picture.

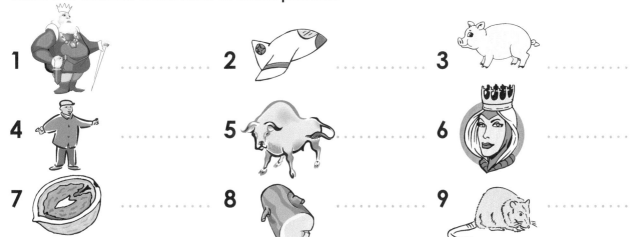

1 .... 2 .... 3 ....

4 .... 5 .... 6 ....

7 .... 8 .... 9 ....

Beginning Sounds 3

Write the missing letter and the whole word again twice.

s for sun ......un ....

t for tap ......ap ....

u for umbrella ......mbrella ....

v for van ......an ....

w for wig ......ig ....

x for x-ray ......-ray ....

y for yacht ......acht ....

z for zebra ......ebra ....

Write the correct word next to each picture.

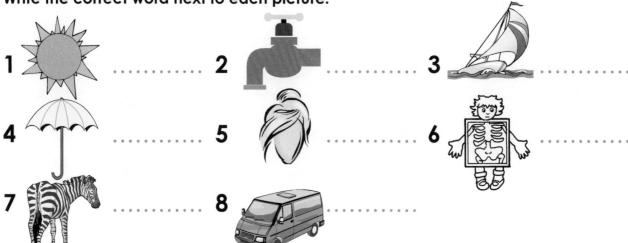

1 .... 2 .... 3 ....

4 .... 5 .... 6 ....

7 .... 8 ....

Put in the letter 'a', then write the whole word again twice.

 b . . . . . g . . . .

 c . . . . . p . . . .

 m . . . . . t . . . .

 j . . . . . m . . . .

 p . . . . n . . . .

 c . . . . n . . . .

Write the correct word next to each picture.

1 . . . . **2** . . . . **3** . . . .

4  . . . . **5** . . . . **6** . . . .

Write 'yes' or 'no' after each sentence.

7   Can a pan nag?   . . . .

8   Can a man be sad?   . . . .

9   Has a cat a cap?   . . . .

Short Vowel Sound 'e'

Put in the letter 'e', then write the whole word again twice.

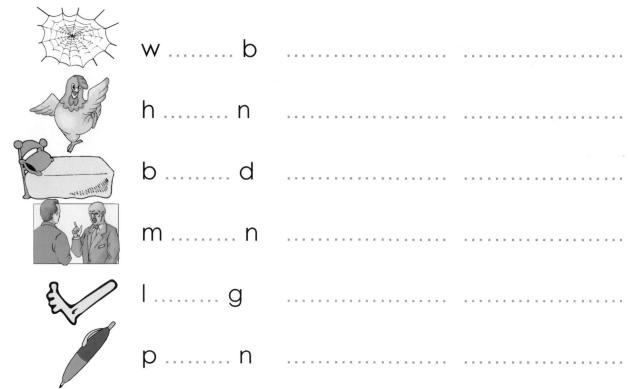

w . . . . b . . . .

h . . . . n . . . .

b . . . . d . . . .

m . . . . n . . . .

l . . . . g . . . .

p . . . . n . . . .

Write the correct word next to each picture.

1 . . . . 2 . . . . 3 . . . .

4 . . . . 5 . . . . 6 . . . .

Write 'yes' or 'no' after each sentence.

7 Can a hen have eggs? . . . .

8 Can a peg be red? . . . .

9 Do men have ten legs? . . . .

    © Peter Howard 2011   Published by Coroneos Publications

Put in the letter 'i', then write the whole word again twice.

t . . . . n . . . .

z . . . . p . . . .

p . . . . n . . . .

b . . . . b . . . .

b . . . . n . . . .

6 s . . . . x . . . .

Write the correct word next to each picture.

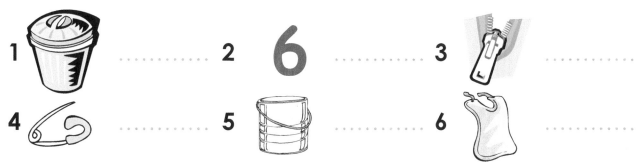

1 . . . .   2 **6** . . . .   3 . . . .

4 . . . .   5 . . . .   6 . . . .

Write 'yes' or 'no' after each sentence.

7 Has a pig a rib?   . . . .

8 Can a tin jig?   . . . .

9 Can a pin sit?   . . . .

Short Vowel Sound 'o'

Put in the letter 'o', then write the whole word again twice.

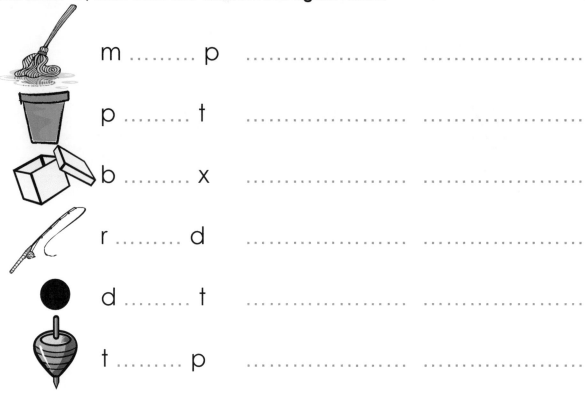

m .... p ....

p .... t ....

b .... x ....

r .... d ....

d .... t ....

t .... p ....

Write the correct word next to each picture.

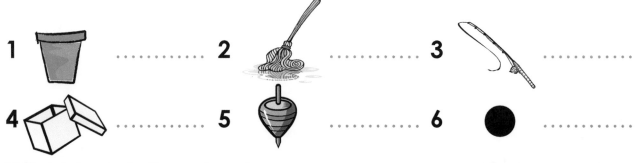

1 .... 2 .... 3 ....

4 .... 5 .... 6 ....

Write 'yes' or 'no' after each sentence.

7   Can a fox sit on a log?   ....

8   Can a mop sob?   ....

9   Is a hog a pig?   ....

    © Peter Howard 2011   Published by Coroneos Publications

Put in the letter 'u', then write the whole word again twice.

r .... g

h .... t

m .... g

t .... b

b .... g

b .... n

Write the correct word next to each picture.

1 .... 2 .... 3 ....

4 .... 5 .... 6 ....

Write 'yes' or 'no' after each sentence.

7 Is the sun hot? ....

8 Can a bun run? ....

9 Can Mum hug? ....

Blending with 'a'

Put in the letter 'a', then write the whole word again twice.

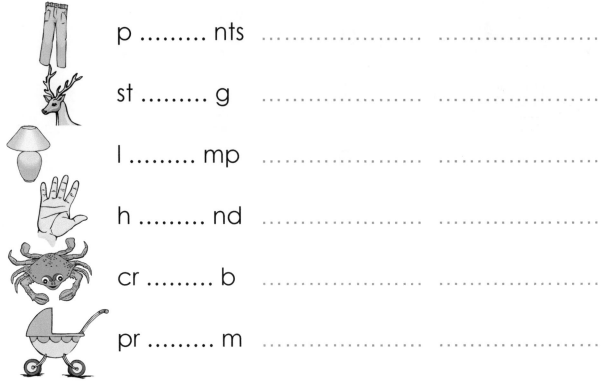

p .... nts ....

st .... g ....

l .... mp ....

h .... nd ....

cr .... b ....

pr .... m ....

Write the correct word next to each picture.

1 .... 2 .... 3 ....

4 .... 5 .... 6 ....

Write 'yes' or 'no' after each sentence.

7   Can a rat be in a trap?   ....

8   Can a flag clap hands?   ....

9   Is there sand on land?   ....

Put in the letter 'e', then write the whole word again twice.

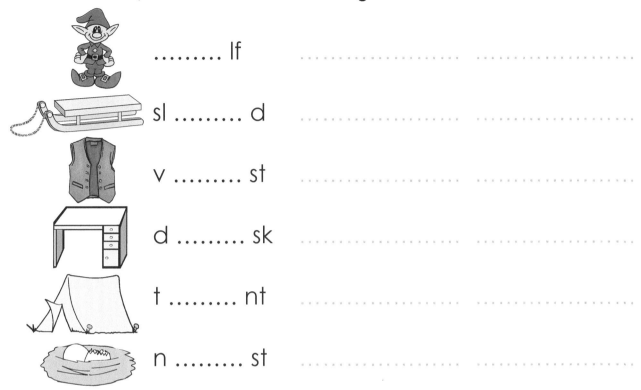

.... lf   ....

sl .... d   ....

v .... st   ....

d .... sk   ....

t .... nt   ....

n .... st   ....

Write the correct word next to each picture.

1 ....   2 ....   3 ....

4 ....   5 ....   6 ....

Write 'yes' or 'no' after each sentence.

7   Can a bug be a pest?   ....

8   Can a pup yelp?   ....

9   Can you bend a leg?   ....

Blending with 'i'

Put in the letter 'i', then write the whole word again twice.

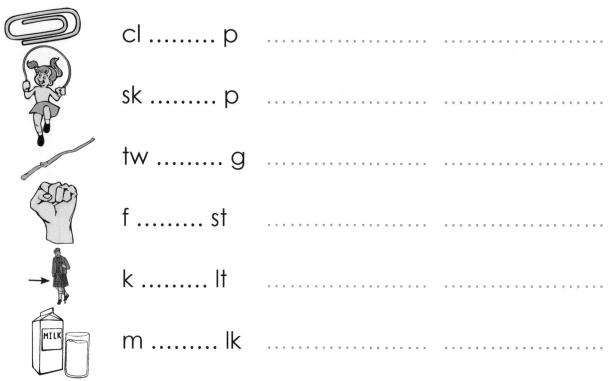

cl .... p ....

sk .... p ....

tw .... g ....

f .... st ....

k .... lt ....

m .... lk ....

Write the correct word next to each picture.

1 .... 2 .... 3 ....

4 .... 5 .... 6 ....

Write 'yes' or 'no' after each sentence.

7   Can a twin skip?   ....

8   Will a top spin?   ....

9   Will a tap drip?   ....

    © Peter Howard 2011   Published by Coroneos Publications

Put in the letter 'o', then write the whole word again twice.

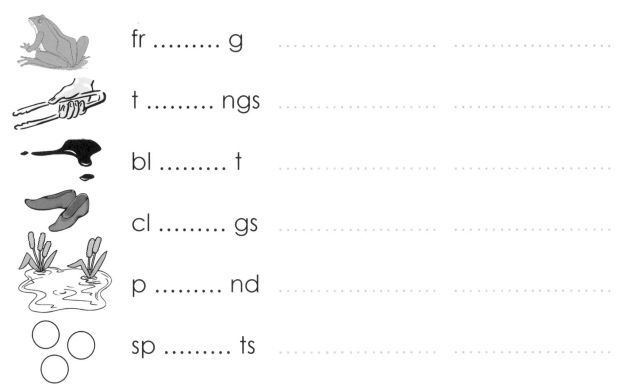

fr .... g   ....

t .... ngs   ....

bl .... t   ....

cl .... gs   ....

p .... nd   ....

sp .... ts   ....

Write the correct word next to each picture.

1 .... 2 .... 3 ....

4 .... 5 .... 6 ....

Write 'yes' or 'no' after each sentence.

7   Can a dog have spots? ....

8   Can a doll trot?   ....

9   Can a pup romp?   ....

Blending with 'u'

Put in the letter 'u', then write the whole word again twice.

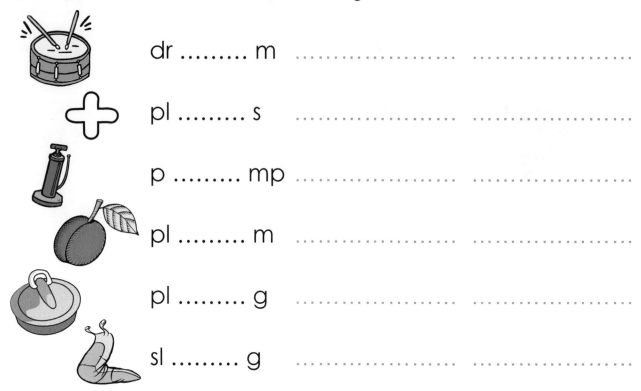

dr .... m ....

pl .... s ....

p .... mp ....

pl .... m ....

pl .... g ....

sl .... g ....

Write the correct word next to each picture.

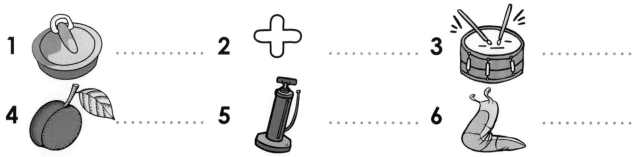

1 .... 2 .... 3 ....

4 .... 5 .... 6 ....

Write 'yes' or 'no' after each sentence.

7 Can a slug jump? ....

8 Can an axe be blunt? ....

9 Is a plump hen fat? ....

Put in the letter 'ck', then write the whole word again twice.

ro ....

pi ....

clo ....

fro ....

tru ....

so ....

Write the correct word next to each picture.

1 .... **2** .... **3** ....

4 .... **5** .... **6** ....

Write 'yes' or 'no' after each sentence.

7 Can you put a brick in a sack? ....

8 Can a pack be on your back? ....

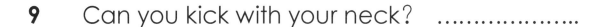

9 Can you kick with your neck? ....

'ch' 'sh' 'th' and 'wh' Sounds

Put in these letters, then write the whole word again twice.

wit......... ....

.... ip ....

.... ong ....

.... ale ....

fi ....

mo ....

Write the correct word next to each picture.

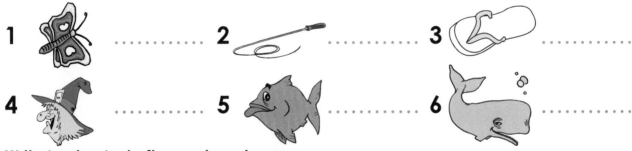

1 ....   2 ....   3 ....

4 ....   5 ....   6 ....

Write 'yes' or 'no' after each sentence.

7 Is a rash lots of spots?   ....

8 Can you have chips for lunch?   ....

9 Can you give a chicken mash?   ....

Put in the letter 'a', then write the whole word again twice.

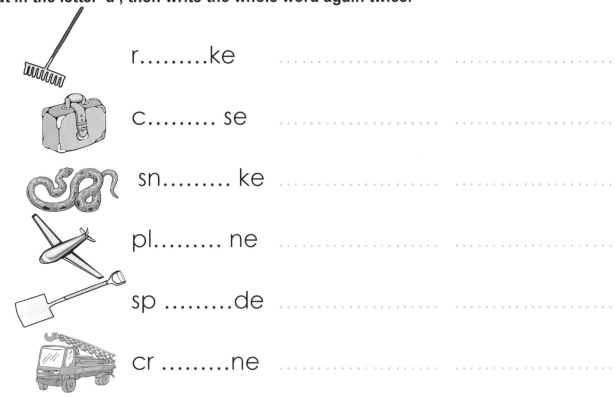

r........ke   ....

c........ se   ....

sn........ ke   ....

pl........ ne   ....

sp ....de   ....

cr ....ne   ....

Write the correct word next to each picture.

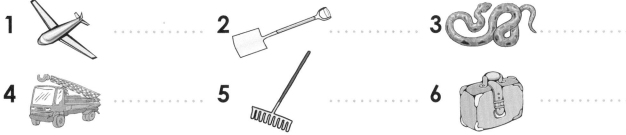

1 .... 2 .... 3 ....

4 .... 5 .... 6 ....

Write 'yes' or 'no' after each sentence.

7   Can you taste a cake?   ....

8   Is a male duck a drake? ....

9   Is a black face pale?   ....

Long Vowel 'i'

Put in the letter 'i', then write the whole word again twice.

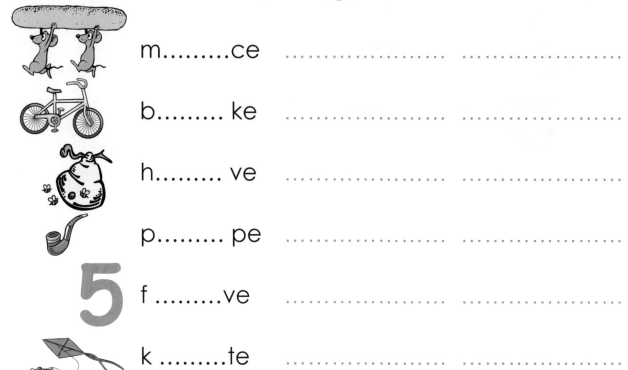

m.........ce ....

b......... ke ....

h......... ve ....

p......... pe ....

f ....ve ....

k ....te ....

Write the correct word next to each picture.

1 .... 2 .... 3 ....

4 .... 5 .... 6 ....

Write 'yes' or 'no' after each sentence.

7   Can bells chime?   ....

8   Is nine less than ten?   ....

9   Can you slide on ice?   ....

Put in the letter 'o', then write the whole word again twice.

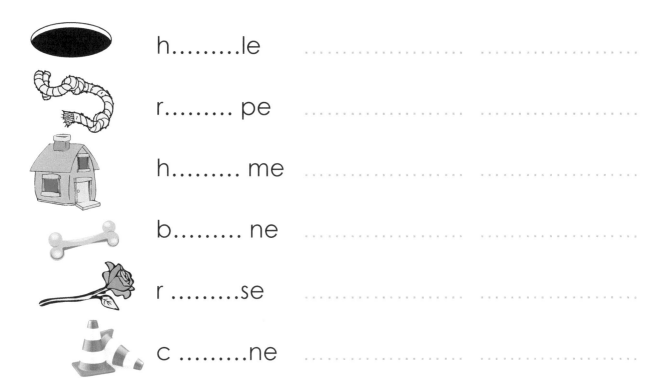

h………le   ....

r……… pe   ....

h……… me   ....

b……… ne   ....

r ………se   ....

c ………ne   ....

Write the correct word next to each picture.

1 ....   2 ....   3 ....

4 ....   5 ....   6 ....

Write 'yes' or 'no' after each sentence.

7   Do dogs like to be stroked?   ....

8   Can you dig a hole with a spade?   ....

9   Can a stone doze in bed?   ....

Long Vowel 'u'

Put in the letter 'u', then write the whole word again twice.

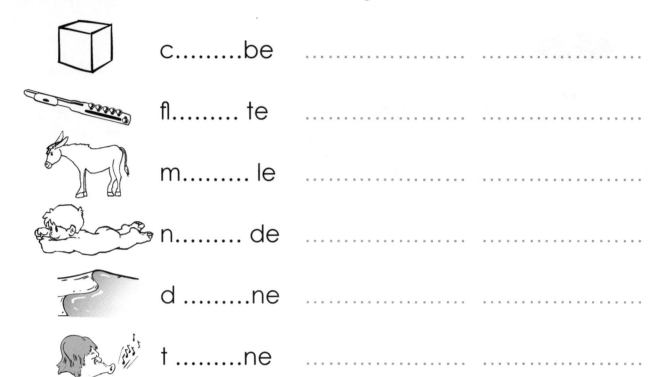

c.........be   ....

fl......... te   ....

m......... le   ....

n........ de   ....

d ....ne   ....

t ....ne   ....

Write the correct word next to each picture.

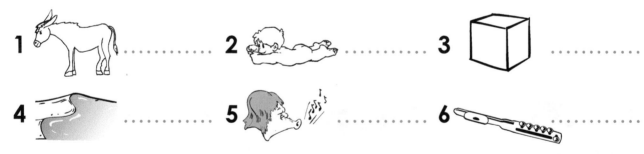

1   2   3   ....

4   5   6   ....

Write 'yes' or 'no' after each sentence.

7   Can a king rule?   ....

8   Do mothers think babies are cute?   ....

9   Can a hat have a plume?   ....

    © Peter Howard 2011   Published by Coroneos Publications

Put in the letters 'ee', then write the whole word again twice.

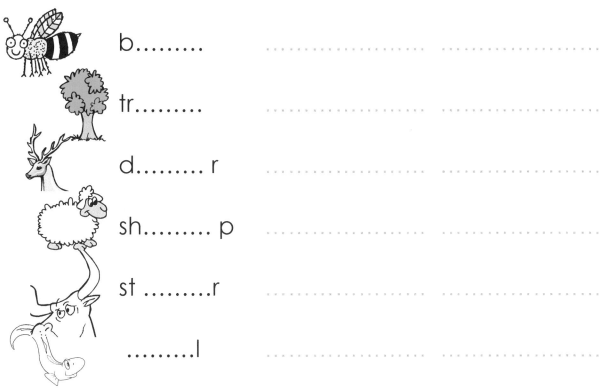

b……… ………………………… …………………………

tr……… ………………………… …………………………

d……… r ………………………… …………………………

sh……… p ………………………… …………………………

st ………r ………………………… …………………………

………l ………………………… …………………………

Write the correct word next to each picture.

1 ………………… 2 ………………… 3 …………………

4 ………………… 5 ………………… 6 …………………

Write 'yes' or 'no' after each sentence.

7   Do sheep feed on steel?   …………………

8   Can you sweep with a brush?   …………………

9   Can a cat drive a jeep? …………………

Published by Coroneos Publications

Revision 'ee' Sound

Complete each word using 'ee' and any missing letter or letters.

1 You can get b.............. or chops

at the butcher's shop.

2 Your h..............s are at the back

of your f..............   .

3 Long e..............s live in the

deep cr..............   .

4 The qu.............. is having a sleep.

5 This t.............. came from

a s.............. .

Put in the letters 'ea', then write the whole word again twice.

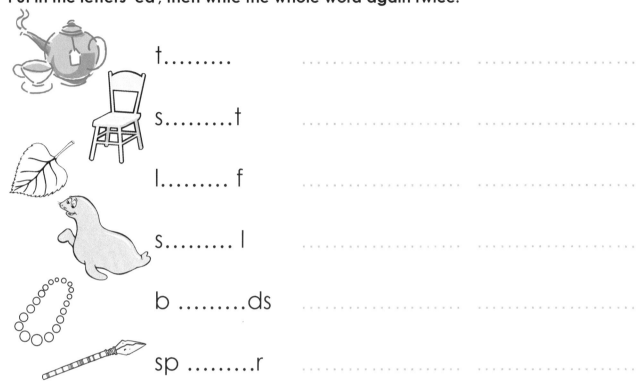

t......... ....

s.........t ....

l......... f ....

s........ l ....

b ....ds ....

sp ....r ....

Write the correct word next to each picture.

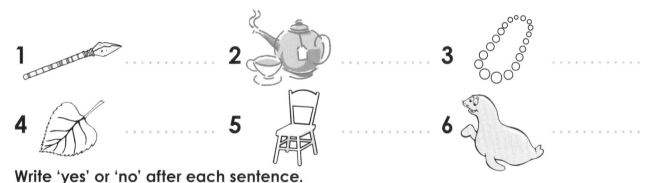

1 .... 2 .... 3 ....

4 .... 5 .... 6 ....

Write 'yes' or 'no' after each sentence.

7   Can a stream run into the sea?   ....

8   Does an eagle eat meat?   ....

9   Can you have a peach at a meal?   ....

Revision 'ea' Sound

Complete each word using 'ea' and any missing letter or letters.

1 The baby let out a sc...............

when she heard the bells p.............. .

2 Cl.............. the knife and put it

back in its sh.............. .

3 She has a home n.............. the

b.............. so we can go for a swim.

4 The man with a b.............. had a dog

on a l..............h.

5 Pl.............. may I have a cup of

w.............. t.............. with lots of milk.

Put in the letters 'oo', then write the whole word again twice.

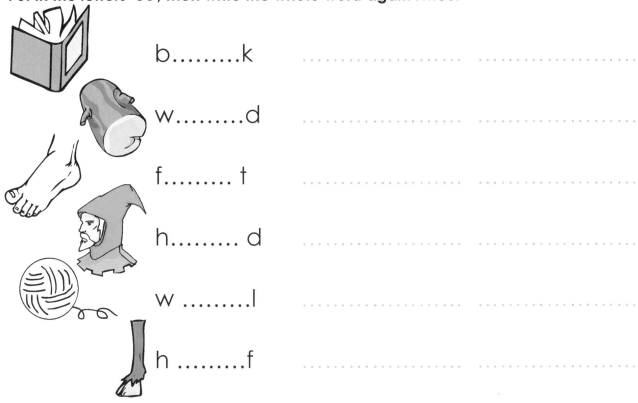

b........k ....

w........d ....

f........t ....

h........d ....

w ....l ....

h ....f ....

Write the correct word next to each picture.

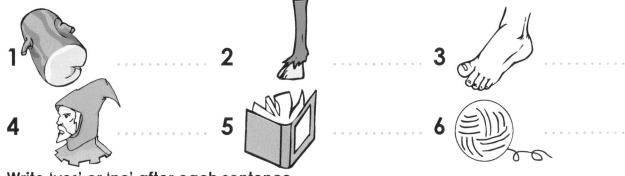

1 .... 2 .... 3 ....

4 .... 5 .... 6 ....

Write 'yes' or 'no' after each sentence.

7   Can you fish in a brook? ....

8   Do we call hens chooks?   ....

9   Will a dog go 'woof woof'? ....

Revision Short 'oo'

Complete each word using 'oo' and any missing letter or letters.

1 The wind sh............. the tree

and leaves fell.

2 Mum says it is g............. to read

b............. .

3 Tammy st............. on a seat

to l............. over the wall.

4 The man who t.............the money

wore a black h.............

5 Mum is c.............ing with a pan

on the stove.

Answers

EXCELLENCE IN ENGLISH BOOK 1

Page

6 Beginning Sounds 1
1 egg **2** ant **3** dog **4** cat **5** fan **6** gun **7** ink **8** hat **9** bus

7 Beginning Sounds 2
1 king **2** jet **3** pig **4** man **5** ox **6** queen **7** nut **8** log **9** rat

8 Beginning Sounds 3
1 sun **2** tap **3** yacht **4** umbrella **5** wig **6** x-ray **7** zebra **8** van

9 Short Vowel Sound 'a'
1 cap **2** mat **3** pan **4** bag **5** jam **6** can **7** no **8** yes **9** no

10 Short Vowel Sound 'e'
1 men **2** web **3** bed **4** leg **5** hen **6** pen **7** yes **8** yes **9** no

11 Short Vowel Sound 'i'
1 bin **2** six **3** zip **4** pin **5** tin **6** bib **7** yes **8** no **9** no

12 Short Vowel Sound 'o'
1 pot **2** mop **3** rod **4** box **5** top **6** dot **7** yes **8** no **9** yes

13 Short Vowel Sound 'u'
1 bun **2** bug **3** tub **4** rug **5** hut **6** mug **7** yes **8** no **9** yes

14 Blending with 'a'
1 stag **2** lamp **3** crab **4** pants **5** pram **6** hand **7** yes **8** no **9** yes

15 Blending with 'e'
1 tent **2** desk **3** vest **4** nest **5** elf **6** sled **7** yes **8** yes **9** yes

16 Blending with 'i'
1 kilt **2** clip **3** twig **4** fist **5** skip **6** milk **7** yes **8** yes **9** yes

17 Blending with 'o'
1 frog **2** blot **3** spots **4** tongs **5** clogs **6** pond **7** yes **8** no **9** yes

18 Blending with 'u'
1 plug **2** plus **3** drum **4** plum **5** pump **6** slug **7** no **8** yes **9** yes

Answers

19 Ending with 'ck'
1 clock **2** rock **3** sock **4** pick **5** frock **6** truck **7** yes **8** yes **9** no

20 'ch' 'sh' 'th' and 'wh' Sounds
1 moth **2** whip **3** thong **4** witch **5** fish **6** whale **7** yes **8** yes **9** yes

21 Long Vowel 'a'
1 plane **2** spade **3** snake **4** crane **5** rake **6** case **7** yes **8** yes **9** no

22 Long Vowel 'i'
1 hive **2** mice **3** pipe **4** kite **5** bike **6** five **7** yes **8** yes **9** yes

23 Long Vowel 'o'
1 rope **2** cone **3** home **4** rose **5** hole **6** bone **7** yes **8** yes **9** no

24 Long Vowel 'u'
1 mule **2** nude **3** cube **4** dune **5** tune **6** flute **7** yes **8** yes **9** yes

25 Double Sound 'ee'
1 steer **2** bee **3** sheep **4** eel **5** tree **6** deer **7** no **8** yes **9** no

26 Revision 'ee' Sound
1 beef **2** heels, feet **3** eels, creek **4** queen **5** tree, seed

27 Double Sound 'ea'
1 spear **2** tea **3** beads **4** leaf **5** seat **6** seal **7** yes **8** yes **9** yes

28 Revision 'ea' Sound
1 scream, peal **2** Clean, sheath **3** near, beach **4** beard, leash **5** Please, weak, tea

29 Short Double Sound 'oo'
1 wood **2** hoof **3** foot **4** hood **5** book **6** wool **7** yes **8** yes **9** yes

30 Revision Short 'oo'
1 shook **2** good, books **3** stood, look **4** took, hood **5** cooking

31 Long Double Sound 'oo'
1 shoot **2** spoon **3** boot **4** moon **5** noon **6** broom **7** yes **8** yes **9** no

32 Revision Long 'oo' Sound
1 droop **2** shoot **3** kangaroo, zoo **4** tooth, food **5** stool, cool

  © Peter Howard 2011 Published by Coroneos Publications

Answers

33 Double Sound 'oa'
1 cloak 2 goal 3 coat 4 toast 5 boat 6 toad 7 yes 8 yes 9 yes

34 Revision 'oa' Sound
1 soap 2 float 3 load, coal 4 roast 5 foal, road

35 Double Sound 'ow'
1 bowl 2 mow 3 crow 4 blow 5 bow 6 snow 7 no 8 yes 9 no

36 Revision 'ow' Sound
1 yellow 2 bowl 3 grow, row 4 grow, sown 5 slowly, low

37 Double Sound 'or'
1 thorn 2 torch 3 fork 4 fort 5 corn 6 cork 7 no 8 yes 9 yes

38 Revision 'or' Sound
1 stork 2 port, storms 3 short 4 horns 5 Pork, sort

39 Double Sound 'aw'
1 hawk 2 claw 3 drawer 4 bawl 5 prawn 6 yawn 7 yes 8 no 9 yes

40 Revision 'aw' Sound
1 yawn 2 crawl 3 draw 4 fawn 5 shawl

41 Double Sound 'ou'
1 trout 2 couch 3 cloud 4 house 5 scout 6 mouse 7 yes 8 no 9 yes

42 Revision 'ou' Sound
1 count 2 mouth 3 round 4 sour 5 loud

43 Double Sound 'ow'
1 towel 2 flower 3 cow 4 sow 5 clown 6 shower 7 yes 8 no 9 yes

44 Revision 'ow' Sound
1 gown 2 crown 3 howl 4 town 5 drown

45 Double Sound 'ar'
1 harp 2 star 3 card 4 tart 5 arm 6 jar 7 yes 8 no 9 no

46 Revision 'ar' Sound
1 snarl 2 cart 3 dark 4 park 5 farm

47 Double Sound 'ai'
1 snail 2 chain 3 paint 4 jail 5 train 6 mail 7 yes 8 yes 9 yes

Answers

48 Revision 'ai' Sound
1 rails **2** sail **3** nail **4** tail **5** rain

49 Double Sound 'ay'
1 sting-ray **2** tray **3** day **4** x-ray **5** hay **6** spray **7** no **8** no **9** yes

50 Revision 'ay' Sound
1 pay **2** bray **3** stray **4** stay **5** clay

51 Double Sound 'ir'
1 shirt **2** circus **3** first **4** bird **5** skirt **6** girl **7** yes **8** yes **9** yes

52 Revision 'ir' Sound
1 third **2** birthday **3** thirsty **4** squirt **5** dirty

53 Double Sound 'ur'
1 burn **2** fur **3** church **4** nurse **5** surf **6** turkey **7** no **8** yes **9** yes

54 Revision 'ur' Sound
1 burnt **2** curly **3** hurt **4** burst **5** urn

55 Double Sound 'er'
1 letter **2** finger **3** tiger **4** river **5** fern **6** dinner **7** yes **8** yes **9** yes

56 Revision 'er' Sound
1 herd **2** jerk **3** butcher **4** flowers **5** slippers

57 Harder Words 1
1 son **2** month **3** front **4** won **5** read **6** bread, steak **7** break **8** swan
9 want, watch **10** wasp

58 Harder Words 2
1 bull **2** pull **3** push **4** bush **5** path, grass **6** raft **7** board **8** roar **9** soar **10** oar

59 Harder Words 3
1 small **2** halt **3** salt **4** ball **5** pearl **6** learn **7** earth **8** dwarf **9** warm **10** warn

60 Harder Words 4
1 wear **2** tear **3** bear **4** pear **5** calm **6** calf **7** half **8** heart **9** pie **10** door

Put in the letters 'oo', then write the whole word again twice.

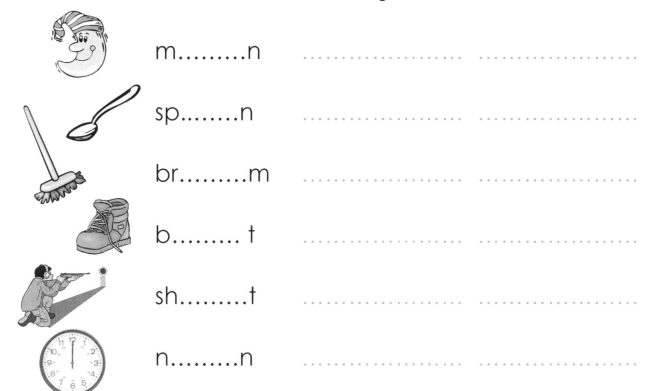

m.........n ....

sp.......n ....

br.........m ....

b......... t ....

sh.........t ....

n.........n ....

Write the correct word next to each picture.

1 .... 2 .... 3 ....

4 .... 5 .... 6 ....

Write 'yes' or 'no' after each sentence.

7   Is a spoon a kind of tool?   ....

8   Can a plane loop the loop?   ....

9   Do hens roost in a room with you?   ....

Revision Long 'oo' Sound

Complete each word using 'oo' and any missing letter or letters.

1   Old flowers in a vase dr...............

2   You can sh............... a ball at a hoop.

3   I saw a kanga.............. at

the z................ .

4   A t.................. is used to

bite f.................. .

5   She sat on a st.................... and

drank iced water to keep c................... .

Put in the letters 'oa', then write the whole word again twice.

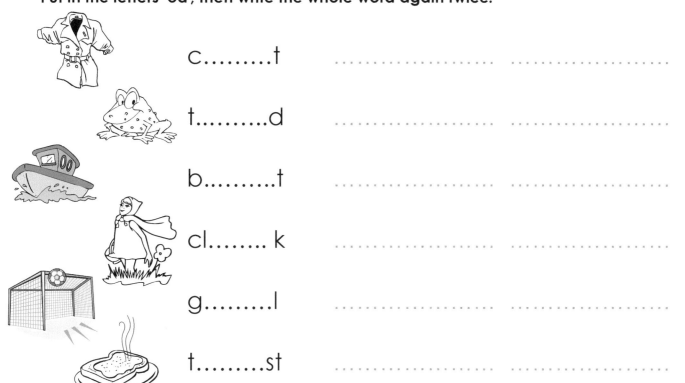

c.........t ....

t.........d ....

b.........t ....

cl........ k ....

g.........l ....

t.........st ....

Write the correct word next to each picture.

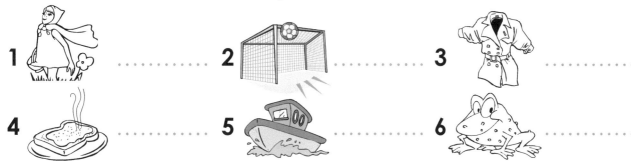

1 .... **2** .... **3** ....

4 .... **5** .... **6** ....

Write 'yes' or 'no' after each sentence.

7 Will a goat eat oats? ....

8 Is the sea at the coast? ....

9 Can you have a sore throat? ....

Revision 'oa' Sound

Complete each word using 'oa' and any missing letter or letters.

1 I wash with s…………………

in the bath.

2 The boat will fl………………… on the pond.

3 The truck has a l………………

of c……………… .

4 I like to eat r……………… beef.

5 The baby f……………… was

on the r……………… .

Put in the letters 'ow', then write the whole word again twice.

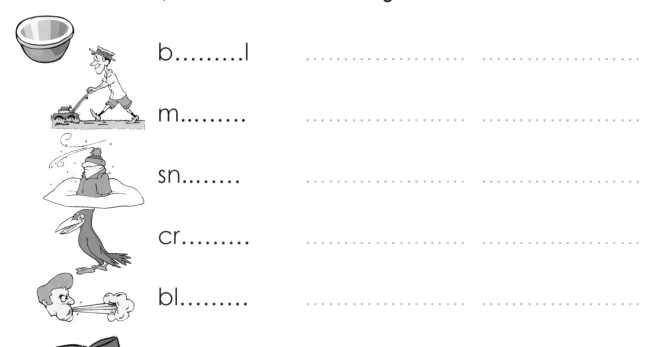

b........l ....

m........ ....

sn........ ....

cr........ ....

bl........ ....

b......... ....

Write the correct word next to each picture.

1 .... 2 .... 3 ....

4 .... 5 .... 6 ....

Write 'yes' or 'no' after each sentence.

7   Can a crow throw a ball?   ....

8   Did men shoot with bows and arrows? ....

9   Is your elbow below your knee? ....

Revision 'ow' Sound

Complete each word using 'ow' and any missing letter or letters.

1 A lemon has ye…..…..……….… skin.

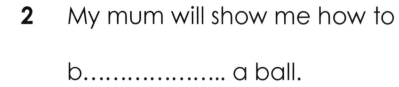

2 My mum will show me how to

b……….………….. a ball.

3 When I g……….…………. up

I will r……….………. a boat.

4 To g……….……….. corn, seeds

must be s……….……….. .

5 To land, a plane s……….…………ly

comes down l……….……….. .

Put in the letters 'or', then write the whole word again twice.

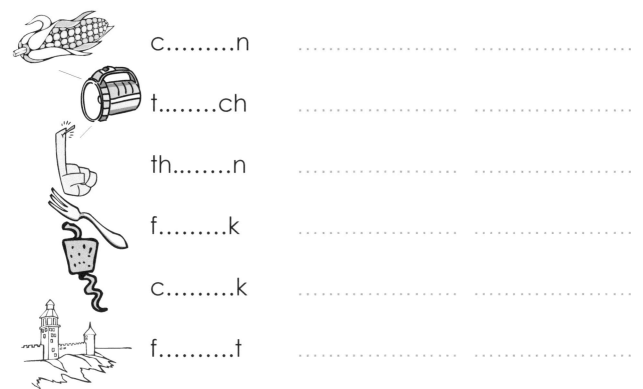

c.........n ....

t.......ch ....

th.......n ....

f........k ....

c........k ....

f.........t ....

Write the correct word next to each picture.

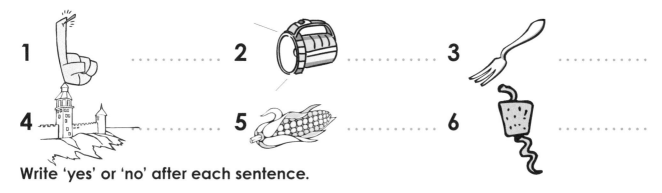

1 .... 2 .... 3 ....

4 .... 5 .... 6 ....

Write 'yes' or 'no' after each sentence.

7   Is it hot at the North Pole?   ....

8   Can a pig grunt and snort?   ....

9   Are sheep shorn for wool?   ....

Revision 'or' Sound

Complete each word using 'or' and any missing letter or letters.

1 A st….................……… is a bird that

wades in water.

2 Ships are safe in p…....................…

from st….................…..s.

3 A Shetland pony is very sh…..................… .

4 Cars long ago had h…....................…

that you squeezed.

5 P…..............… is a s…..............… of meat

we get from pigs.

Put in the letters 'aw', then write the whole word again twice.

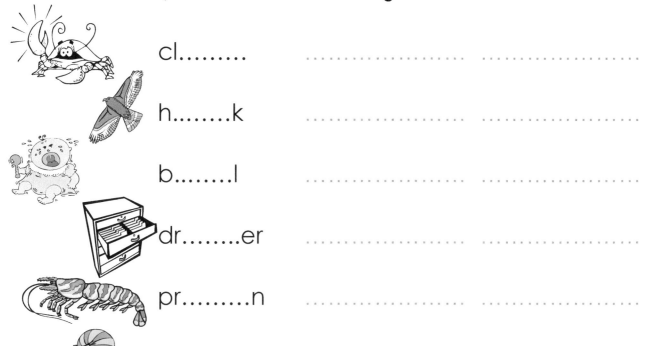

cl.........

h.......k

b........l

dr.......er

pr.........n

y ....

Write the correct word next to each picture.

1 ....

2 ....

3 ....

4 ....

5 ....

6 ....

Write 'yes' or 'no' after each sentence.

7   Do lawns need mowing?   ....

8   Do you eat straw in the mornings?   ....

9   Has a cat paws?   ....

Revision 'aw' Sound

Complete each word using 'aw' and any missing letter or letters.

1 We y......................... when

we are tired.

2 A baby must cr..........................

before he or she can walk.

3 I use a pencil to d...................... .

4 A f......................... is a baby deer.

5 My grannie wears

a sh.................. .

    © Peter Howard 2011   Published by Coroneos Publications

Put in the letters 'ou', then write the whole word again twice.

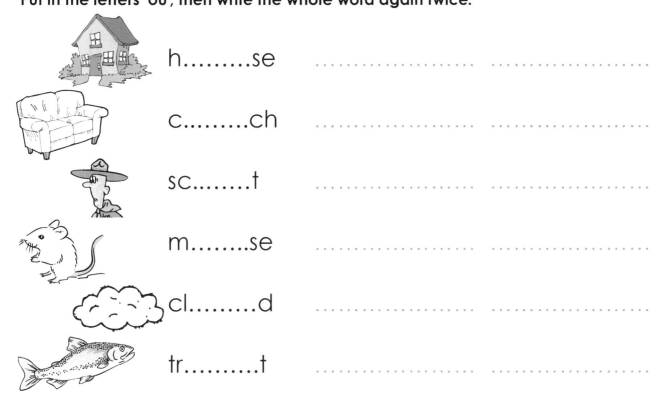

h.........se ....

c.........ch ....

sc.........t ....

m.........se ....

cl.........d ....

tr.........t ....

Write the correct word next to each picture.

1 .... 2 .... 3 ....

4 .... 5 .... 6 ....

Write 'yes' or 'no' after each sentence.

7   Do your ears pick up sounds?   ....

8   Is a rugby ball round?   ....

9   Has a pig a snout?   ....

Revision 'ou' Sound

Complete each word using 'ou' and any missing letter or letters.

1 I can c...................... to ten on

my fingers.

2 A bird's m......................... is

a beak.

3 A tennis ball is r...................... .

4 A lemon tastes s......................... .

5 Some dogs have a

l................... bark.

      © Peter Howard 2011   Published by Coroneos Publications

Put in the letters 'ow', then write the whole word again twice.

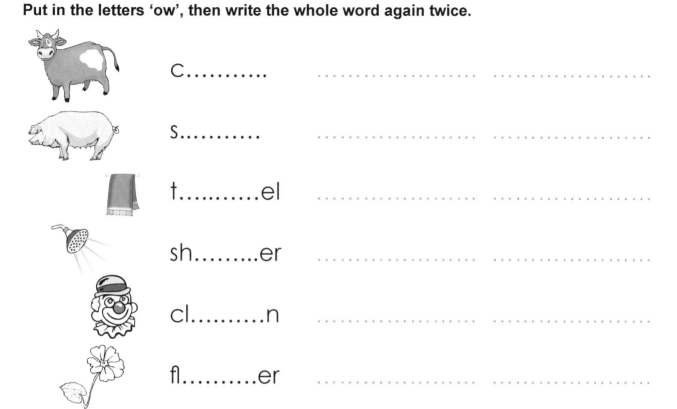

c………..   …………………………   …………………………

s………..   …………………………   …………………………

t………el   …………………………   …………………………

sh……..er   …………………………   …………………………

cl………n   …………………………   …………………………

fl………er   …………………………   …………………………

Write the correct word next to each picture.

1 …………   2 …………   3 …………

4 …………   5 …………   6 …………

Write 'yes' or 'no' after each sentence.

7   Is a hen a fowl?   ………………..

8   Do we eat owls?   ………………..

9   Can a cow be brown?   ………………..

Revision 'ow' Sound

Complete each word using 'ow' and any missing letter or letters.

1 Mum wore a green g......................

to the ball.

2 The king has a c........................

on his head.

3 Last night I heard a dog h...................... .

4 There are lots of houses in

a t................ .

5 Do not swim alone in a pool

as you may dr.................. .

Put in the letters 'ar', then write the whole word again twice.

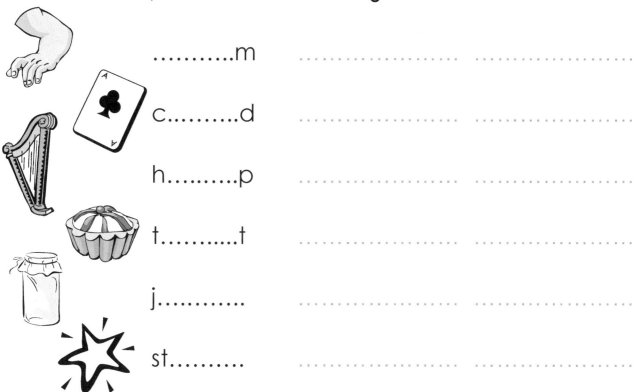

..........m

c..........d

h..........p

t..........t

j..........

st..........

Write the correct word next to each picture.

1 .... 2 .... 3 ....

4 .... 5 .... 6 ....

Write 'yes' or 'no' after each sentence.

7 Do sharks bite? ....

8 Is a blunt knife sharp? ....

9 Can a cat bark like a dog? ....

Revision 'ar' Sound

Complete each word using 'ar' and any missing letter or letters.

1   Some dogs sn…….….………… .

2   The farmer had a horse

and c………………t.

3   At night it gets d…………………… .

4   There are swings in the

p……………..   .

5   On a f……………….. there are

sheep and cows.

Double Sound 'ai'

Put in the letters 'ai', then write the whole word again twice.

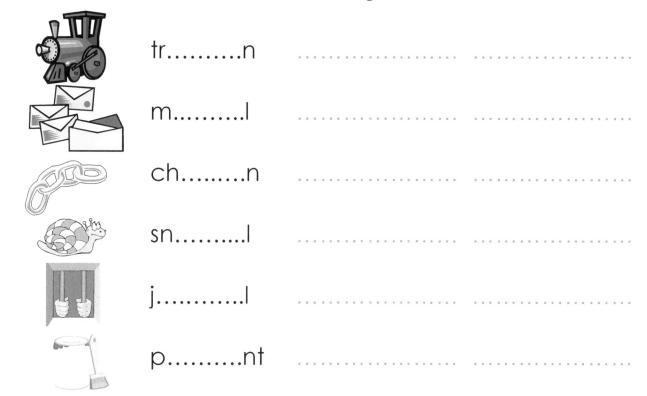

tr.........n ....

m.........l ....

ch........n ....

sn.........l ....

j..........l ....

p.........nt ....

Write the correct word next to each picture.

1 .... 2 .... 3 ....

4 .... 5 .... 6 ....

Write 'yes' or 'no' after each sentence.

7   Does a belt go round your waist? ....

8   Does hail fall from the sky? ....

9   Do we use bait to catch fish? ....

Revision 'ai' Sound

Complete each word using 'ai' and any missing letter or letters.

1   A train runs on r…..…..…………   .

2   This boat uses the wind

to s………………   .

3   You can hit a n…………………

with a hammer.

4   A happy dog wags its t……………...

5   You get wet if you stand in

the r……………...   .

Put in the letters 'ay', then write the whole word again twice.

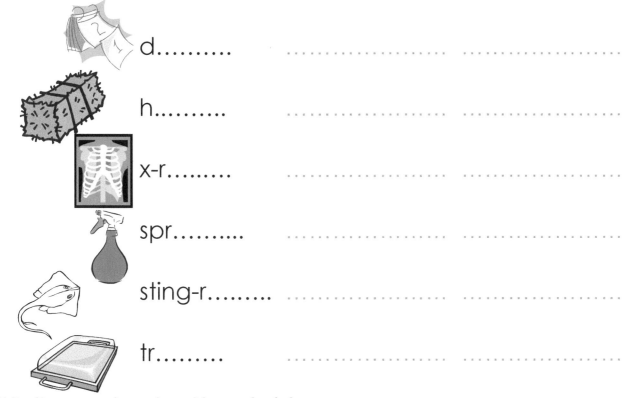

d.......... ....

h.......... ....

x-r......... ....

spr.......... ....

sting-r......... ....

tr......... ....

Write the correct word next to each picture.

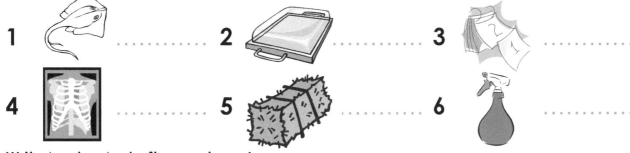

1 ....   2 ....   3 ....

4 ....   5 ....   6 ....

Write 'yes' or 'no' after each sentence.

7 Do babies play with snakes? ....

8 Does 'stay' mean go away? ....

9 Can a crow lay eggs? ....

Revision 'ay' Sound

Complete each word using 'ay' and any missing letter or letters.

1   You have to p….....…………… for

things you buy in shops.

2   Cows moo and donkeys

b…………………… .

3   A dog with no home is

a st………………. .

4   On a long car trip you can

s……………….. at a motel.

5   Garden pots are made from c………………. .

Put in the letters 'ir', then write the whole word again twice.

g........l ....

sk........t ....

sh........t ....

c.........cus ....

f.........st ....

b........d ....

Write the correct word next to each picture.

1 .... 2 .... 3  ....

4 .... 5  .... 6 ....

Write 'yes' or 'no' after each sentence.

7 Can a baby bird chirp? ....

8 Can you stir with a spoon? ....

9 Is a birch a kind of tree? ....

Revision 'ir' Sound

Complete each word using 'ir' and any missing letter or letters.

1 I came th..................... in my race.

2 It is her b.....................day today.

3 A person who is th.................y

needs a drink.

4 My pistol can sq.................

water.

5 Take a shower if you are d....................y.

Put in the letters 'ur', then write the whole word again twice.

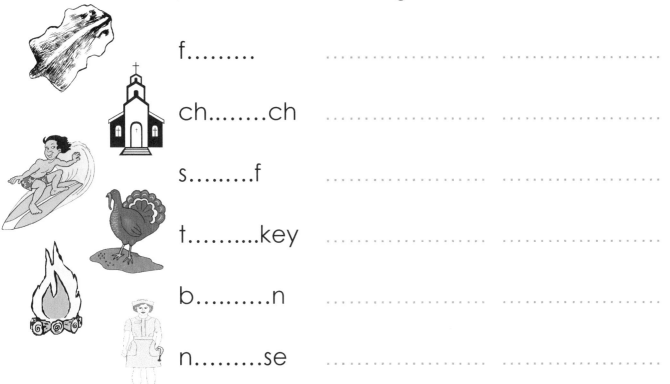

f......... ....

ch.......ch ....

s.........f ....

t.........key ....

b..........n ....

n.........se ....

Write the correct word next to each picture.

1 .... 2 .... 3 ....

4 .... 5 .... 6 ....

Write 'yes' or 'no' after each sentence.

7   Do cats purr when they are angry? ....

8   Will a baby burp after drinking milk? ....

9   Do the wheels of a car turn? ....

Revision 'ur' Sound

Complete each word using 'ur' and any missing letter or letters.

1 Do not stay out in the sun or

you will get b......................t.

2 This little girl has c......................y

hair.

3 This little boy has h.................

his arm.

4 The cat will make the balloon

b.................t.

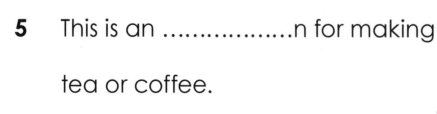

5 This is an ....n for making

tea or coffee.

Excellence in English Year 1

Put in the letters 'er', then write the whole word again twice.

tig……… ……………… ………………

riv……… ……………… ………………

f………n ……………… ………………

dinn……… ……………… ………………

lett……… ……………… ………………

fing……… ……………… ………………

Write the correct word next to each picture.

1 ……………… 2 ……………… 3 ………………

4 ……………… 5 ……………… 6 ………………

Write 'yes' or 'no' after each sentence.

7   Can a bird sit on a perch?   ………………

8   Do we eat herbs?   ………………

9   Do we wait at a kerb to cross a road?   ………………

Revision 'er' Sound

Complete each word using 'er' and any missing letter or letters.

1 A h…………….. of cows was on

the road.

2 When I was fishing I felt my

line j………………… .

3 A but……………….. sells meat.

4 Some flo……………….grow in

this garden.

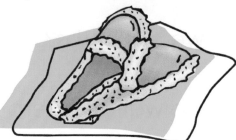

5 Inside the house I put on my

slip……………..s.

Harder Words 1

These words have irregular sounds. Write the correct one in each space using the words in the boxes.

son   won   front   month

1 Mr Jones has a .... called Jack.

2 June is a winter .... in Australia.

3 A porch is at the .... of a hou

4 I .... my race at school.

bread   read   break   steak

5 I once .... a book about a wicked

witch.

6 At lunch I ate .... and ....

7 It is easy to .... a glass.

want   wasp   watch   swan

8 A .... is a large bird.

9 I .... a new .... as a present.

10 A .... is an insect that stings.

Harder Words 2

These words have irregular sounds. Write the correct one in each space using the words in the boxes.

bull	bush	push	pull

1   A .... is a father cow.

2   A car can .... a caravan.

3   Mum will .... the baby in a pram.

4   The bird made a nest in the ....

raft	path	grass

5   Walk on the .... and keep off the ....

6   A .... will float on water.

oar	roar	soar	board

7   The teacher writes on the ....

8   A lion can ....

9   A bird can .... in the sky.

10 An .... is used to row a boat.

© Peter Howard 2011   Published by Coroneos Publications

Harder Words 3

These words have irregular sounds. Write the correct one in each space using the words in the boxes.

	salt	ball	halt	small

1   A tall person is not ……………………….. .

2   To stop is to …………………… .

3   I like to put …………………………. on my food.

4   Can you catch a …………………….. ?

	learn	pearl	earth

5   Mum has a ………………………. ring.

6   I like to ………………………. at school.

7   Plants grow in the …………………….. .

	warm	dwarf	warn

8   A ……………………………….. is a very small person.

9   It is …………………… by the fire.

10   The sign is there to …………………………. swimmers.

Harder Words 4

These words have irregular sounds. Write the correct one in each space using the words in the boxes.

bear	wear	pear	tear

1   I like to ……………………… nice shoes.

2   It is easy to ……………………… clothes on barbed wire.

3   A ……………………… is a strong animal.

4   A ……………………….. is a tasty fruit.

calf	calm	half

5   To stay ……………………….. is to not get angry.

6   A ……………………… is a baby cow.

7   We each ate ………………………… an apple.

door	heart	pie

8   Your ………………………. beats all the time.

9   I like to eat a meat ………………… .

10   Please open the ……………………..… and let me in.